DUDLEY SCHOOLS
LIBRARY SERVICE

first book of
bikes
and motorbikes

Isabel Thomas

KU-453-191

Schools Library and Information Services

S00000772252

For Harry, Joey and Oscar

Published 2014 by
A&C Black
An imprint of Bloomsbury Publishing Plc
50 Bedford Square, London, WC1B 3DP

www.bloomsbury.com

ISBN 978-1-4081-9459-1

Copyright © 2014 Bloomsbury Publishing Plc
Text copyright © 2014 Isabel Thomas
Illustrations: Jean-Michel Girard

The right of Isabel Thomas to be identified as the author of
this work has been asserted by her in accordance with the
Copyrights, Designs and Patents Act 1988.

A CIP catalogue for this book is available from the British Library.

All rights reserved. No part of this publication may be
reproduced in any form or by any means – graphic, electronic
or mechanical, including photocopying, recording, taping or
information storage and retrieval systems – without the prior
permission in writing of the publishers.

This book is produced using paper that is made from wood
grown in managed, sustainable forests. It is natural, renewable
and recyclable. The logging and manufacturing processes
conform to the environmental regulations of the country of origin.

Printed in China by C&C.

10 9 8 7 6 5 4 3 2 1

DUDLEY PUBLIC LIBRARIES

L

772252   Sd

J629.227

Contents

Bike and Motorbike safety
Motorbikes are powerful machines. They can be very dangerous.
Always have an adult with you when you look at bikes or
motorbikes. Do not touch bikes or motorbikes. Do not stand
close to roads. Make sure cyclists and riders can see you.

Bikes and motorbikes

Bikes and motorbikes are vehicles with two wheels. Look out for people pedalling speedy racing bikes and tough mountain bikes. Listen out for the roar of motorbike engines.

You can spot bikes and motorbikes riding on and off the road. You can also find out what they used to look like at museums. This book will help you to name the bikes and motorbikes you see.

At the back of this book is a Spotter's Guide to help you remember the bikes and motorbikes you see. Tick them off as you spot them. You can also find out the meaning of some useful words here.

Turn the page to find out all about bikes and motorbikes!

Road bike

Bikes like this are easy to ride on roads. They can carry us to school or work. People also use them for exercise, exploring, and fun.

Cyclists push the pedals with their feet. This turns a chain, which turns the back wheel.

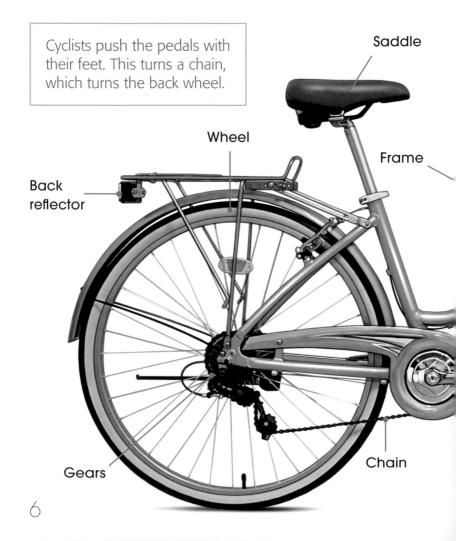

Saddle

Wheel

Frame

Back reflector

Gears

Chain

The handlebars move the front wheel left or right to steer the bike.

Postal workers and messengers use bikes to make deliveries.

Bell

Handlebars

Brake lever

Basket to carry goods

Brake

Front reflector

Spoke

Pedal

Tyre

Mountain bike

This tough bike is made for off-road adventures. It can bump over rocky ground, climb steep hills, and slide down muddy trails.

You can spot mountain bikes on roads too. They are some of the most popular bikes.

Gears help cyclists ride up hills more easily.

Mudguard

Gear lever

Forks with suspension

Strong frame

Wide tyres

Deep tread

Tandem bike

Two people work together to ride a tandem bike. Both cyclists pedal, but only the front rider steers.

Look out for tandems being used in paracycling races.

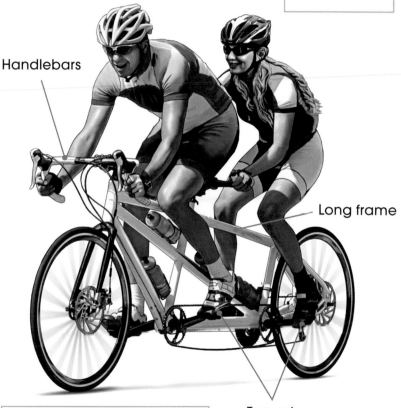

Handlebars

Long frame

Two sets of pedals

The riders have to work as a team to balance the bike.

Unicycle

Unicycles have just one wheel. There are no handlebars or brakes! They are difficult to ride. Some riders learn to balance so well they can ride off-road, or perform tricks.

Comfortable saddle

Frame

Pedal

Tyre

Spokes

Sports like hockey and basketball can be played on unicycles. Riders have both hands free.

Unicycle riders have to pedal downhill.

Recumbent bike

Could you ride a bike lying down? Recumbent bikes have seats shaped like chairs. Riders lie back with their legs out in front. This is very comfortable.

Recumbent bikes are good for cycling long distances. It is easy to travel fast.

Handlebars

Pedal

Large seat

Recumbent bikes are safer for people who have injuries.

Racing bike

Racing bikes are very speedy. Riders bend over the low handlebars. This helps them to travel faster.

Racing bikes like this take part in road races.

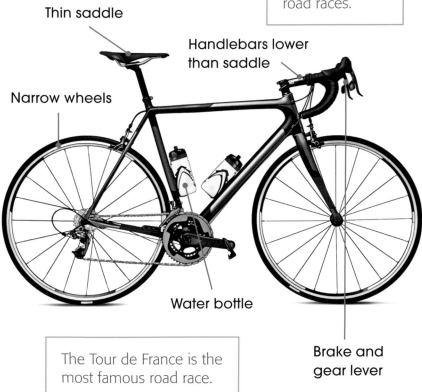

Thin saddle

Handlebars lower than saddle

Narrow wheels

Water bottle

Brake and gear lever

The Tour de France is the most famous road race.

This racing bike is used for time trials. A time trial is a race. Riders try to get the fastest time.

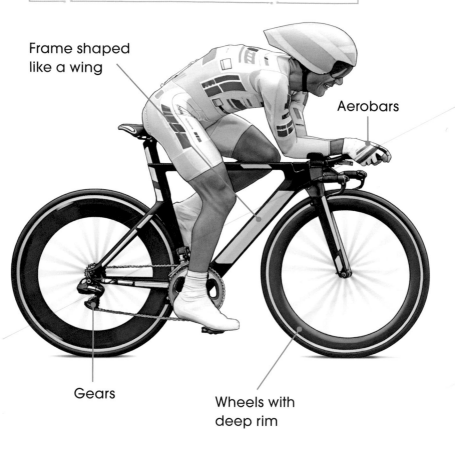

Frame shaped
like a wing

Aerobars

Gears

Wheels with
deep rim

At top speed, riders rest their arms
on the aerobars. Tucking their arms
in helps them to go even faster.

Track racing bike

This bike races at velodromes.
These are oval tracks with steep
sides. Riders do not have to slow
down as they go around bends.

High saddle

There are many
different track races,
including short sprints.

Handlebars

Disc covers
rear spokes

Light, hard
wheels

Track bikes do not have brakes. Riders
slow down by pedalling more slowly.

Monowheel

The rider sits inside a monowheel. The pedals turn smaller wheels, which make the large wheel roll along the ground.

Monowheels are difficult to balance. They are mainly used for fun. You might spot one at a special event.

Outer wheel

Handlebars

Saddle

Inner wheel

Pedal

BMX bike

BMX racers roll and jump around bumpy tracks. BMX freestyle riders do tricks on the ground, on obstacles, or in the air!

A gyro lets the handlebars turn all the way around without tangling the brake cable.

Freestyle bikes need strong, heavy frames. Riders stand on them to do tricks.

Riders stand on these pegs when they do tricks

Saddle

Gyro

Short, strong frame

Pedal

Small, wide wheels

Smooth tyres

BMX racers wear goggles and helmets that cover their face.

One brake

Low seat

121

121

Long, light frame

Small wheels help this BMX race bike to speed up quickly.

Tricycle

A tricycle has three wheels. This makes balancing easy. In many cities, tricycle taxis called trishaws carry passengers and deliver goods.

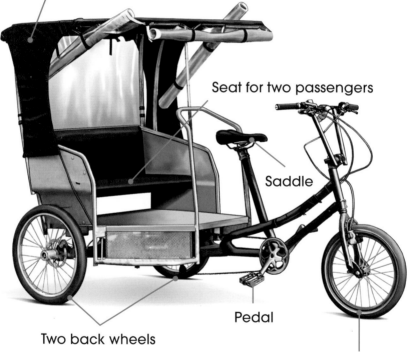

Folding hood

Seat for two passengers

Saddle

Two back wheels

Pedal

One front wheel

Trishaws are very popular in Asia but you can spot them in cities around the world, including London.

Folding bike

This bike folds up at the end of a journey. It can be carried like a suitcase. It fits easily on buses and trains, or in a car boot.

Many people use folding bikes to travel to work.

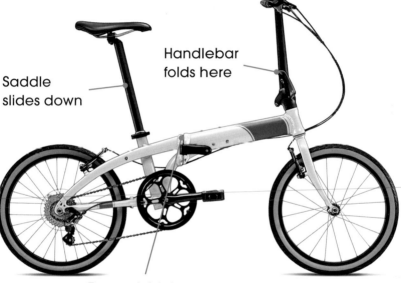

Saddle slides down

Handlebar folds here

Frame folds here

Folding the bike takes around 20 seconds.

Folding pedal

Handcycle

Handcycle riders turn the chain with their hands rather than their feet. There are handgrips instead of pedals. Most handcycles have three wheels, to help riders balance.

Riders kneel or sit back on the seat.

Handgrips

Seat

Chain

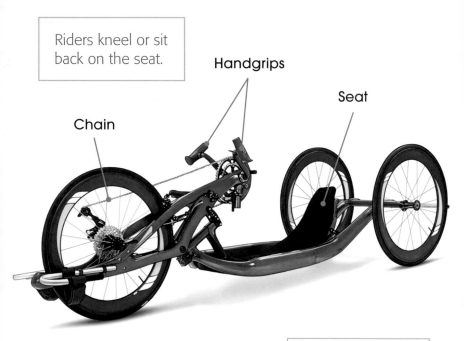

Look out for handcycles being used in paracycling races.

Vintage bike

People have been riding bikes for almost 200 years. Look out for very old bikes in museums.

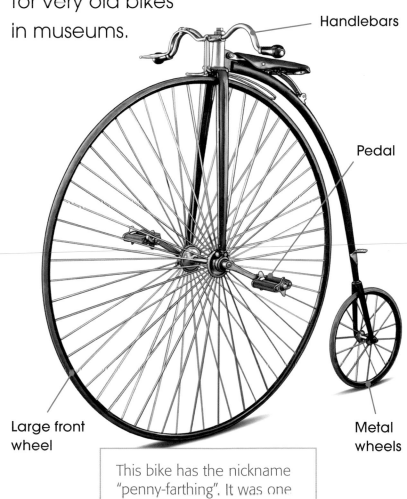

Handlebars

Pedal

Large front wheel

Metal wheels

This bike has the nickname "penny-farthing". It was one of the first bikes with pedals.

Street motorbike

Street motorbikes are popular in towns and cities. They can dodge traffic in crowded streets. The rider turns the throttle to speed up, and squeezes the brakes to slow down.

Saddle

Fuel tank

Exhaust

A motorbike's engine turns the back wheel using a chain.

Covered chain

Handlebar

Throttle

Brake

Riders steer
by turning the
handlebars left or
right. They also
lean into corners,
to stop the
motorbike from
flipping over.

Headlight

Indicator light

Forks

Engine   Tyre

Sport motorbike

Powerful engines help sport motorbikes to travel fast. They have a smooth shape to move through the air quickly. Riders lean forwards and tuck their legs in so their body shape is smooth too.

Helmets and tough clothes protect riders if they fall or crash.

Helmet

Visor

Throttle

Clothes made of tough material

Brake

Padded boots

Tough gloves

Dirt bike

Dirt bikes can ride over grass, mud, sand, and rocks. They are used for getting around the countryside, off-road racing, and exciting stunts.

In some off-road races, riders have to cross obstacles quickly.

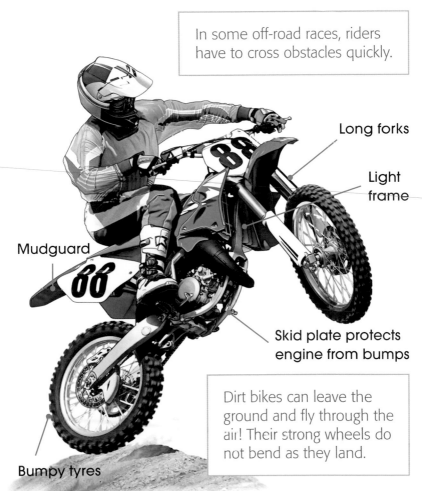

Long forks

Light frame

Mudguard

Skid plate protects engine from bumps

Dirt bikes can leave the ground and fly through the air! Their strong wheels do not bend as they land.

Bumpy tyres

Speedway motorbike

These speedy off-road bikes have powerful engines and no brakes. They skid and slide around oval racetracks covered in dirt.

Riders from different teams race each other to collect points.

Helmet

Goggles

Powerful engine

No brakes

Classic motorbike

New motorbikes are designed every year. But some riders prefer to ride motorbikes that were popular in the past. Some of these classic motorbikes are almost 100 years old.

Many classic bikes were made in the 1930s, 1940s, or 1950s.

High saddle

Fuel tank

Large shiny engine

Owners restore classic bikes to keep them working properly.

Colourful paint

 # Cruiser

Cruisers are new motorbikes that are built to look like classic motorbikes. They have large, powerful engines and travel fast.

Riders sit back in the seat with their feet stretched out in front.

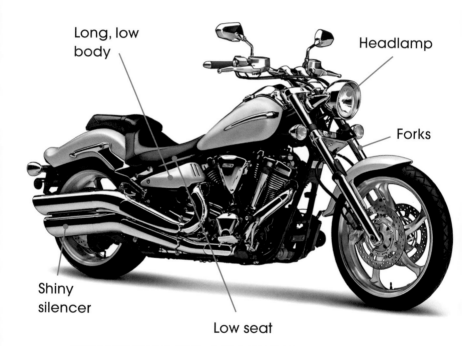

Long, low body

Headlamp

Forks

Shiny silencer

Low seat

The silencer stops exhaust gases making a loud noise as they rush out of the engine.

Touring motorbike

Tourers are the biggest motorbikes. They are as heavy as small cars. Large fuel tanks and powerful engines make them good for long journeys.

Luggage is carried in special boxes at the back and sides.

Radio aerial

Passenger seat

Large windscreen

Rider seat

Giant engine

Luggage boxes

Headlights

Tourers have comfortable seats for two people. They can also carry passengers in a sidecar.

 # Chopper

Some riders change or 'customise' their motorbikes. They add or take away parts to make them look or work better. Customised motorbikes are known as 'choppers'.

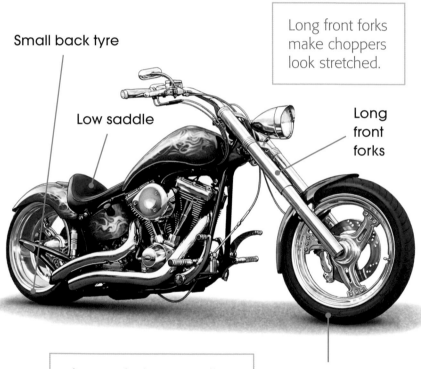

Small back tyre

Low saddle

Long front forks make choppers look stretched.

Long front forks

Large front tyre

The panels that normally cover the engine and frame have been taken off.

Scooter

Look out for scooters zipping around towns and cities. The low frame means that riders can step on and off easily.

Scooters have small engines that are good for short journeys.

Legshields

Compartment to store luggage or helmet

Small wheels

Legshields stop the front wheel from flicking water on the rider.

 # Quad bike

Quad bikes have motorbike engines and controls, but four wheels like a car. They can travel over all types of ground, such as mud, snow, and sand, without getting stuck.

Quad bikes are also called all-terrain vehicles (ATVs).

Seat

Rack to carry equipment

Handlebars

Mudguard

Suspension

Chunky tyres

Quad bikes are useful for people who work on mud or sand.

Sidecar

Sidecars help motorbikes carry extra passengers or luggage. Look out for sidecars joined to large touring motorbikes. You can also watch racing sidecars zoom around a speedway track.

A sidecar stops the motorbike from leaning into bends. The rider turns the handlebars to turn corners.

Rider

Handle for passenger to hold on to

Passenger

The passenger leans to the side to stop the sidecar from flipping over as it goes around bends.

Emergency motorbike

Police, firefighters, and paramedics use motorbikes to get to emergencies quickly.

A siren and flashing lights warn other vehicles to clear the road.

Flashing lights

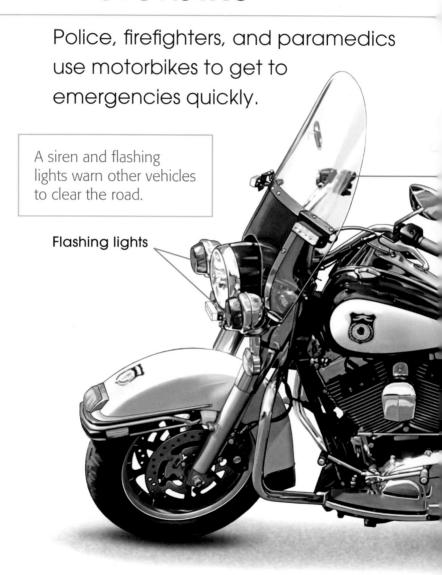

Motorbikes can travel through busy traffic faster than cars and vans.

Flashing light

Radio to keep in touch with base

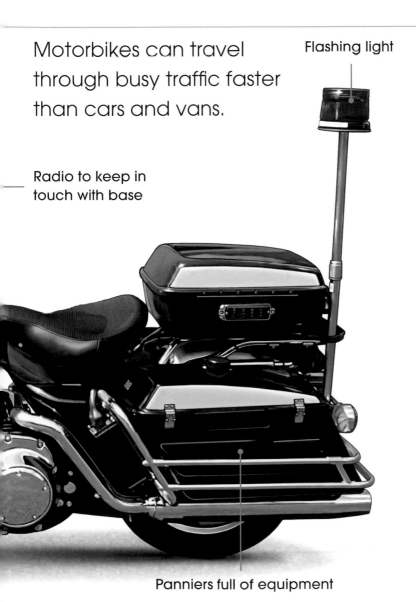

Panniers full of equipment

Superbike

Superbikes are the fastest motorbikes allowed on normal roads. They look and work just like racing superbikes.

Rounded tyres grip the road as the rider turns corners.

Panels cover the engine

Headlight

Engine

Indicator light

Superbikes have powerful engines but very light bodies, to go as fast as possible.

Racing superbike

This superbike was designed just for racing. It tours the world, taking part in a competition called the Moto Grand Prix World Championship.

MotoGP superbikes can travel as fast as 340 km/h.

Race suit made of kangaroo leather

Knee slider

Smooth shape

Powerful engine

Riders lean to the side to help the motorbikes speed around corners. Tough kneepads protect their knees if they touch the track.

Slick tyres with no tread

Motor tricycle

Three wheels make it easy to balance. Trike riders do not have to put their feet on the floor when they stop.

Motor tricycles are safer than normal motorbikes.

Luggage compartment under seat

Front wheels tilt to help the trike turn corners

Some motor tricycles have two wheels at the back and one at the front.

Dragster

Dragsters are the most powerful motorbikes. They race along short, straight tracks. Two or three engines help a dragster get to 370 km/h.

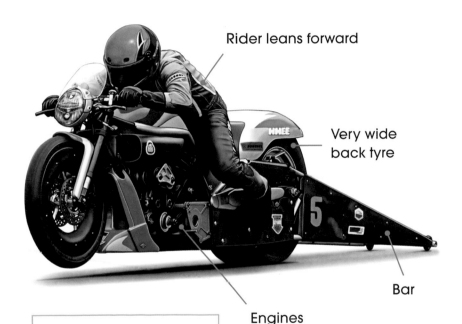

Rider leans forward

Very wide back tyre

Bar

Engines

The front wheel lifts off the track as the dragster speeds up. Bars at the back stop the motorbike from flipping over.

Electric motorbike

Most motorbikes have petrol engines. This motorbike has an electric motor instead. Electric motorbikes are much quieter than normal motorbikes.

Electric motorbikes do not make exhaust fumes. They help to keep the air clean.

Motor

Large batteries

No exhaust pipe

This is an electric racing motorbike.

Useful words

engine a machine that burns fuel to make a motorbike go

exhaust a pipe that carries heat and fumes away from an engine

frame the main piece of a bike or motorbike that holds the other parts together

forks poles that connect the front wheel of a bike or motorbike to the frame

suspension springs and shock absorbers inside the forks that make the ride smoother as a bike or motorbike goes over bumps

paracycling cycling sports for athletes with physical disabilities

throttle a device that controls how much fuel flows into an engine

tread the part of a tyre marked with grooves, that grips the road

tyre the soft rubber that covers bike and motorbike wheels

Spotter's guide

How many of these bikes and
motorbikes have you seen?
Tick them when you spot them.

☐ Road bike
page 6

☐ Mountain
bike
page 8

☐ Tandem bike
page 9

☐ Unicycle
page 10

Recumbent
bike

Racing bike

Time trial
bike

Track racing
bike

Monowheel

BMX freestyle
bike

☐ **BMX race bike**
page 17

☐ **Tricycle**
page 18

☐ **Folding bike**
page 19

☐ **Handcycle**
page 20

☐ **Vintage bike**
page 21

☐ **Street motorbike**
page 22

Sport motorbike
page 24

Dirt bike
page 25

Speedway motorbike
page 26

Classic motorbike
page 27

Cruiser
page 28

Touring motorbike
page 29

 Chopper
page 30

Scooter
page 31

 Quad bike
page 32

Sidecar
page 33

 Emergency
motorbike
page 34

Superbike
page 36

 Racing superbike
page 37

 Motor tricycle
page 38

 Dragster
page 39

Electric motorbike
page 40

Find out more

If you would like to find out more about bikes and motorbikes, you could visit a transport museum. These websites are a good place to start.

National Cycle Museum
www.cyclemuseum.org.uk

The National Motorcycle Museum
www.nationalmotorcyclemuseum.co.uk

Haynes International Motor Museum
www.haynesmotormuseum.com